AMERICA'S FAVORITE SYMBOLS

THE BALD EAGLE
OUR NATIONAL EMBLEM

JINNOW KHALID

New York

Published in 2021 by The Rosen Publishing Group, Inc.
29 East 21st Street, New York, NY 10010

First Edition

Portions of this work were originally authored by Maria Nelson and published as *The Bald Eagle*. All new material in this edition authored by Jinnow Kahlid.

Editor: Elizabeth Krajnik
Book Design: Reann Nye

Photo Credits: Cover, p.1 aaltair/Shutterstock.com; Series Art sunwart/Shutterstock.com; p. 5 Allen.G/Shutterstock.com; p. 7 Albert Beukhof/Shutterstock.com; p. 9 Jim Barber/Shutterstock.com; p. 11 https://commons.wikimedia.org/wiki/File:US_Great_Seal_Charles_Thomson_Preliminary_Design.jpg; p. 13 Smith Collection/Gado/Archive Photos/Getty Images; p. 15 Everett Historical/Shutterstock.com; p. 17 John Ceulemans/Shutterstock.com; p. 19 Deo/Shutterstock.com; p. 21 FloridaStock/Shutterstock.com.

Library of Congress Cataloging-in-Publication Data

Names: Khalid, Jinnow, author.
Title: The bald eagle : our national emblem / Jinnow Khalid.
Description: New York : PowerKids Press, [2021]
Identifiers: LCCN 2019043834 | ISBN 9781725317185 (paperback) | ISBN 9781725317208 (library binding) | ISBN 9781725317192 (6 pack) | ISBN 9781725317215 (ebook)
Subjects: LCSH: United States–Seal–Juvenile literature. | Emblems, National–United States–Juvenile literature. | Bald eagle–United States–Juvenile literature. | Animals–Symbolic aspects–Juvenile literature.
Classification: LCC CD5610 .K47 2021 | DDC 929.90973–dc23
LC record available at https://lccn.loc.gov/2019043834

Manufactured in the United States of America

CPSIA Compliance Information: Batch #CSPK20. For Further Information contact Rosen Publishing, New York, New York at 1-800-237-9932.

CONTENTS

National Emblem

The bald eagle is the national **emblem** of the United States. In 1782, Congress **adopted** the Great Seal of the United States. The seal has the image of a bald eagle on it. Bald eagles are a **symbol** of strength.

Beautiful Bird

The American bald eagle is a beautiful bird. This eagle has a mostly brown body, white head and tail, and yellow **beak** and feet. It isn't bald, as in lacking hair. "Bald" can also mean "marked with white."

Coat of Arms

The coat of arms of the United States is on the front of the country's Great Seal. This is a symbol of the government's power. The coat of arms has a bald eagle with a shield on its chest. The eagle holds an olive branch and 13 arrows.

E PLURIBUS
UNUM

Final Design

An eagle didn't appear on a **design** for the coat of arms until May 9, 1782. This exact eagle wasn't used. Another eagle appeared on the final design of the coat of arms. Congress adopted the Great Seal on June 20, 1782.

E PLURIBUS UNUM

Using the Great Seal

The Great Seal appears on many important papers from the United States government. It also appears in and on government buildings across the country. Each year, the government puts about 3,000 seals on official papers. That's a lot of bald eagles!

“A Much More Respectable Bird”

In a letter to his daughter in 1784, Benjamin Franklin questioned the choice of the bald eagle on the Great Seal. He said the bald eagle on the seal looks more like a turkey. He said the turkey is “a much more respectable bird.”

Benjamin Franklin

Bald Eagles on Currency

Eagles have appeared on U.S. currency, or money, since the nation's early years. They've appeared on half-dollar coins, silver dollar coins, and quarters. Since 1935, the American bald eagle has appeared on the back of $1 bills.

UNITED STATES OF AMERICA
E PLURIBUS UNUM
FG
HALF DOLLAR

Fewer Bald Eagles

In 1776, there were perhaps as many as 100,000 **breeding** pairs of bald eagles in the United States. However, by 1963, there were only 417 breeding pairs. There were fewer bald eagles because people hunted them and destroyed their homes.

Growing Numbers

Bald eagle numbers also dropped because of DDT. This is a **poison** people used to spray on plants to keep pests away. In 1940, a law made it illegal to hunt or harm bald eagles. Today, bald eagle numbers are growing again!

Timeline

1776
Congress calls for a United States seal to be designed.

1782
Congress adopts the Great Seal of the United States, which has the image of a bald eagle on it.

1784
Benjamin Franklin questions the choice of the bald eagle for the Great Seal.

1935
The bald eagle first appears on the back of the $1 bill.

1940
Congress passes a law to protect bald eagles.

GLOSSARY

adopt: To accept and put into action.

beak: The hard, usually pointed, parts that cover a bird's mouth.

breed: To produce baby animals.

design: A drawing or plan of something to be made.

emblem: A person or thing that stands for an idea.

poison: A harmful kind of matter that can kill a living thing.

symbol: Something that stands for something else.

INDEX

WEBSITES

Due to the changing nature of Internet links, PowerKids Press has developed an online list of websites related to the subject of this book. This site is updated regularly. Please use this link to access the list: www.powerkidslinks.com/afs/baldeagle